The
Miracle
of the
Eucharist

George E. Pfautsch

authorHOUSE®

AuthorHouse™
1663 Liberty Drive
Bloomington, IN 47403
www.authorhouse.com
Phone: 1 (800) 839-8640

Published by AuthorHouse 03/21/2018

ISBN: 978-1-5462-3446-3 (sc)
ISBN: 978-1-5462-3445-6 (e)

Library of Congress Control Number: 2018903640

Print information available on the last page.

Scriptural passages have been taken from The New American Bible - Saint Joseph Edition and all catechetical passages have been taken from the Catechism of the Catholic Church

CONTENTS

INTRODUCTION

For the past two thousand years, the Eucharist has been the centerpiece of Catholic faith. At the Last Supper our Lord himself presided at the first Eucharist. He concluded the transubstantiation of the bread and wine into his Body and Blood with the words, "Do This in Memory of Me."

With those words our Lord invites all the faithful into a very special Holy Communion with Him. The Eucharist is truly the apex of our faith.

The Catholic Church defines the Eucharist in the following two manners:
1. The Eucharist is the Source and Summit of Ecclesial Life (the reason we gather together at the Mass).
2. The Eucharist is the Sum and Summary of our Faith.

Documents of Vatican II also placed significant emphasis

on the importance of the Eucharist to the Catholic Church:

1. The most Blessed Sacrament contains the Church's entire spiritual wealth.
2. The Eucharist shows itself to be the source and apex of the whole proclamation of the Gospel.

The Church could not be more clear on the important role of the Eucharist to the Catholic faith.

To comprehend the importance of the Eucharist to the Church, one must understand that which the Church states to be the belief of the Eucharist. That belief was underscored at the Council of Trent which was held between the years 1545 and 1563.

At that Council, a reaffirmation was made of what the Church has always believed in regards to the Eucharist. The Catholic Catechism summarizes that reaffirmation made at the Council as follows:

Because Christ our Redeemer said that it was truly his body that he was offering under the species of bread, it has always been the conviction of the Church of God and the Holy Council now declares again, that by the consecration of the bread and wine there takes place a change of the whole substance of the bread into the substance of the body of Christ our Lord and of the whole substance of the wine into the substance of his blood. This change the holy Catholic Church has fittingly and properly called the transubstantiation.

Effectively, the Church is telling us that the Eucharist is a miracle. A miracle is defined as a supernatural event. The transubstantiation of the substance of bread and wine into the body and blood of our Lord is a supernatural event. It is also a beautiful, mystical mystery and a sacrificial memorial of He who died for our salvation. It is how we demonstrate our love of Him. We have no better way to love Him with all our heart, soul, mind and strength as He commanded us to do.

Even though the Eucharist is the apex of the Catholic faith to faithful members of the Church, there are many Christians, including Catholics, who do not view the Eucharist as a miracle. From the time of Christ until the present time many have not and many do not accept the belief that wine and bread can be transubstantiated into the body and blood of our Lord.

During his Discourse on the Bread of Life our Lord summarized his comments as follows:

Amen, amen, I say to you, unless you eat the flesh of the Son of Man and drink his blood, you do not have life within you. Whoever eats my flesh and drinks my blood has eternal life, and I will raise him on the last day. For my flesh is true food, and my blood is true drink.

Many of his disciples, upon hearing his words said, "This saying is hard: who can accept it?", and they no longer followed Him.

The Catholic Church acknowledges the difficulty of those who have found and those who still find it impossible to believe in the true presence of the Body and Blood of our Lord in the Eucharist.

That difficulty is explained as follows in CCC 1336 of the Catholic Catechism:

The first announcement of the Eucharist divided the disciples just as the announcement of the Passion scandalized them: "This is a hard saying, who can listen to it?" The Eucharist and the Cross are stumbling blocks. It is the same mystery and it never ceases to be an occasion of division. "Will you also go away?" the Lord's question echoes through the ages, as a loving invitation to discover that only he has the "words of eternal life" and that to receive in faith the gift of his Eucharist is to receive the Lord himself.

The above words very properly imply that the difficulty is attributable to the depth of our faith. The Eucharist is indeed a barometer of our faith.

In the Nicene Creed we state the belief in an almighty God, but too many of us go forward placing limitations on the word "almighty". Our, "almighty God" possessed the might to create all the galaxies in the universe from nothing. It is no more difficult for that same almighty God to change the nature of something that already exists (bread and wine). It is therefore the limitations of one's faith that restricts the ability of one to believe in the miracle of the Eucharist.

We have already made reference to the transubstantiation of bread and wine into the Body and Blood of our Lord as a miracle. But if we are to view the miracles of the Eucharist more broadly we must also address other divine aspects. It is through the divine prism that we can more broadly understand the power, majesty and miracle of the Eucharist.

The purpose of this book is to provide as many beautiful aspects of the Eucharist as this flawed writer and sinner can present with the understanding that any attempts to fully explain the Eucharist will never be complete. As flawed and sinful humans, none of us will ever be able to completely comprehend the divine and mysterious aspects of the Eucharist. Nevertheless, the divine aspects are part of the miracle of the Eucharist and will also be covered in this book.

CHAPTER 1

BIBLICAL REFERENCES

The Sacrament of the Eucharist was established by Jesus on the night of the Last Supper. The "Institution of the Holy Eucharist" is now celebrated as the Fifth Luminous Mystery of the Holy Rosary.

The institution of the Eucharist was foreshadowed by events in the Old Testament as early as the Book of Genesis. In Chapter 14 we are told the story of Abraham's victory over Cherdorlaomer, the king of Elam, Following that victory, Melchizedek, king of Salem (shalom - meaning king of peace) brought out bread and wine, and being a priest of God most High, he blessed Abram. Melchizedek of whom little is known and to whom no genealogy is assigned, continues to this day to be recognized as the first priest. He is remembered in the famous song, which is sung, at the ordinations and anniversaries of priests to this day.

Our Catechism tells us that, *"The Christian tradition considers Melchizedek, "priest of God Most High," as a prefiguration of the priesthood of Christ, the unique, high priest after the order of Melchizedek", "holy, blameless, unstained," "by a single offering he has perfected for all time those who are sanctified," that is, by the unique sacrifice of the cross.* That redemptive sacrifice on the cross is unique as it was accomplished at one time for all of us, but yet is made present to all of us through the Eucharistic sacrifice in which we can participate at the celebration of each Mass we attend.

There are numerous other prefigurations of Christ and the Eucharist in the Old Testament. The feast of the Passover, which continues to be celebrated by the Jewish people foreshadowed the crucified Body and Blood of Christ via the body and blood of the killing of the lamb.

After the Passover, the Jewish people began their Exodus to the Promised Land. During the Exodus God fulfilled the words he gave to Moses, "I will rain bread (manna) from heaven for you; and the people shall go out and gather a day's portion every day..." Through the bread rained down from heaven we are reminded of the Holy Sacrifice of the Mass and the bread from heaven that nourishes our soul.

There are numerous other ways in which the Old Testament prefigured the coming of Christ and the Eucharist. Bread and wine were often referenced in ways that should remind us of the bread and wine now offered at the Mass to be transubstantiated into the Real Presence of Christ.

But let us move to the New Testament and explore how "The Eucharist shows itself to be the source and apex of the whole proclamation of the Gospel". In doing that we will look especially at the words of our Lord himself.

Our Lord, who has knowledge of all things, understood the difficulties that would accompany the institution of the Holy Eucharist. Nevertheless, He would give us many reasons to believe through a number of actions prior to the Last Supper.

Chapter 14 of Matthew gives us one of his early actions. After Jesus learned of the death of John the Baptist, Verse 13 of Chapter 14 tells the miracle of the loaves and fish.

The Return of the Twelve and the Feeding of the Five Thousand. When Jesus heard of it. (the death of John) *he withdrew to a deserted place by himself. The crowds heard of this and followed him on foot from their towns. When he disembarked and saw the vast crowd, his heart was moved with pity for them, and he cured their sick.*

When it was evening, the disciples approached him and said, "This is a deserted place and it is already late; dismiss the crowds so that they can go to the villages and buy food for themselves." Jesus said to them, "There is no need for them to go away: give them some food yourselves."

But they said to him, "Five loaves and two fish are all we have here." Then he said, Bring them to me," and he ordered the crowds to sit down on the grass. Taking the five loaves and the two fish, and looking up to heaven, he said the blessing, broke the loaves, and gave them to the crowds. They all ate and were satisfied, and they picked up the fragments left over - twelve wicker baskets full.

Those who ate were about five thousand men, not counting women and children.

It is noteworthy that after taking the loaves and fish our Lord looked up to heaven, said the blessing and then broke the loaves. It was an unmistakable action of foreshadowing the Eucharist itself. It was also a powerful miracle, which no doubt bolstered the faith of those present at that time just as the Eucharist should bolster our faith in this generation. Despite the many signs He gave us, many today still find it difficult to believe the miracle of the Eucharist.

On the day after the miracle of loaves and fish, Jesus gave his very special prefiguration of the Eucharist in his Bread of Life Discourse. Because of its importance to our belief in the Real Presence in the Eucharist we will include it in its entirety. It is covered in the sixth chapter of John beginning with verse 22

The Bread of Life Discourse - *The next day, the crowd that remained across the sea saw that there had been only one boat there and that Jesus had not gone along with his disciples in the boat, but only his disciples had left. Other boats came from Tiberias near the place where they had eaten the bread when the Lord gave thanks. When the crowd saw that neither Jesus nor his disciples were there, they themselves got into the boats and came to Capernaum looking for Jesus. And when they found him across the sea they said to him, "Rabbi, when did you get here?"*

Jesus answered them and said, "Amen, amen, I say to you, you are looking for me not because you saw signs but because you ate the loaves and were filled. Do not work for food that perishes but for the food that endures for eternal life, which the Son of Man will give you. For on him the Father, God, has set his seal." So they said to him, "What can we do to accomplish the works of God?" Jesus answered and said to them, "This is the work of God, that you believe in the one he sent."

So they said to him, "What sign can you do, that we may see and believe in you? What can you do? Our ancestors ate manna in the desert, as it is written: 'He gave them bread from heaven to eat. '"

So Jesus said to them, "Amen, amen, I say to you, it was not Moses who gave the bread from heaven; my Father gives you the true bread from heaven." For the bread of God is that which comes down from heaven and gives life to the world."

So they said to him, "Sir, give us this bread always." Jesus said to them, "I am the bread of life; whoever comes to me will never hunger and whoever believes in me will never thirst. But I told you that although you have seen me, you do not believe. Everything that the Father gives me will come to me, and I will not reject anyone who comes to me, because I came down from heaven not to do my will but the will of the one who sent me.

And this is the will of the one who sent me, that I should not lose anything of what he gave me, but that I should raise it on the last day. For this is the will of my Father, that everyone who sees the Son and believes in him may have eternal life, and I shall raise him on the last day."

The Jews murmured about him because he said, "I am the bread that came down from heaven," and they said, "Is this not Jesus, the son of Joseph? Do we not know his father and mother? Then how can he say, "I have come down from heaven?" Jesus answered and said to them "Stop murmuring" among yourselves. No one can come to me unless the Father who sent me draw him, and I will raise him on the last day. It is written in the prophets:

'They shall all be taught by God.'

Everyone who listens to my Father and learns from him comes to me. Not that anyone has seen the Father except the one who is from God; he has seen the Father.

Amen, amen, I say to you, whoever believes in me has eternal life. I am the bread of life. Your ancestors ate the manna in the desert, but they died; this is the bread that comes down from heaven so that one may eat it and not die. I am the living bread that came down from heaven; whoever eats this bread will live forever; and the bread that I will give is my flesh for the life of the world."

The Jews quarreled among themselves, saying, "How can this man give us his flesh to eat?" Jesus said to them, "Amen, amen, I say to you, unless you eat the flesh of the Son of Man and drink his blood, you do not have life within you. Whoever eats my flesh and drinks my blood has eternal life, and I will raise him on the last day. For my flesh is true food, and my blood is true drink. Whoever eats my flesh and drinks my blood remains in me and I in him. Just as the living Father sent me and I have life because of the Father, so also the one who feeds on me will have life because of me. This is the bread that came down from heaven. Unlike your ancestors who ate and still died, whoever eats this bread will live forever." These things he said while teaching in the synagogue in Capernaum.

The Words of Eternal Life - *Then many of his disciples who were listening said, "This saying is hard; who can accept it?" Since Jesus knew that his disciples were murmuring* *about this, he said to them, "Does this shock you? What if you were to see the Son of Man ascending to where he was before? It is the spirit that gives life, while the flesh is of no avail. The words I have spoken to you are spirit and life. But there are some of you who do not believe." Jesus knew from the beginning the ones who would not believe and the one who would betray him. And he said, "For this reason I have told you that no one can come to me unless it is granted him by my Father."*

As a result of this, many of his disciples returned to their former way of life and no longer accompanied him. Jesus then said to the Twelve, "Do you also want to leave?" Simon Peter answered him, "Master to whom shall we go? You have the words of eternal life. We have come to believe and are convinced that you are the Holy One of God." Jesus answered them, "Did I not choose you twelve? Yet is not one of you a devil?" He was referring to Judas, son of Simon the Iscariot; it was he who would betray him, one of the Twelve.

The above words from the Bread of Life Discourse give all of us much on which to meditate and much to discern. Many Christians do not believe in the transubstantiation and only our Lord is capable of judging the interpretation of his words by those who read them. For all my life, my belief has been aligned with the teaching of the Catholic Church, that the Bread and Wine we offer, becomes the Body and Blood of our Lord. Others believe differently and our belief depends on our faith. I further believe that it is the Eucharist which nourishes our soul (the spirit that gives life).

For those of us who believe in the miracle of the transubstantiation, it is difficult for us to understand those who do not believe. For believers, there is great reliance (faith) on our Lord's words that "whoever eats this bread will live forever".

From the earliest days of Christianity, the Eucharist has been celebrated. In the Acts of the Apostles, the breaking of the bread is noted several times. St. Paul, in his many letters, also notes the celebration of the Eucharist in several places in the Bible.

After his Resurrection our Lord walked with two of his disciples on the road from Jerusalem to Emmaus. While they were walking the disciples did not recognize our Lord. As they were approaching the village of Emmaus they urged him to stay with them. The words from Luke 24 go on to tell us - *And it happened that, while he was with them at table, he took the bread, said the blessing broke it and gave it to them. With that their eyes were opened and they recognized him, but he vanished from their sight.*

That passage is of importance as relates to the Eucharist, because it states that "their eyes were opened". The reception of Holy Communion, when received with great faith and fervor, opens our own eyes to greater faith, spiritual wisdom, and holiness, and permits us to share in his divinity.

Even without the teachings of the Church, our Lord's own words in the Bible, should lead us to believing in the spiritual power of the Eucharist.

CHAPTER 2

EUCHARISTIC BELIEFS OF THE CATHOLIC CHURCH

The Eucharistic beliefs of the Catholic Church are beautifully set forth in the Catechism of the Catholic Church which begins with Article 3, Page 334 of the 1994 edition. Near the beginning of Article 3, in paragraph CCC 1313 the Eucharist is described as follows:

At the Last Supper, on the night he was betrayed, our Savior instituted the Eucharistic sacrifice of his Body and Blood. This he did in order to perpetuate the sacrifice of the cross throughout the ages until he should come again, and so to entrust to his beloved Spouse, the Church, a memorial of his death and resurrection: a sacrament of love, a sign of unity, a bond of charity, a Paschal banquet in which Christ is consumed, the mind is filled with grace, and a pledge of future glory is given to us.

To all people of the Catholic faith, as well as those interested in the Catholic faith, I strongly urge you to read the entire Article 3, "The Sacrament of the Eucharist", in the Catechism. If we wish to understand the Catholic faith we need to understand the importance of the Eucharist to that faith.

Following CCC 1323, the Catechism begins the first section with the heading, "The Eucharist - Source and Summit of Ecclesial Life". That heading underscores the importance of the Eucharist to the Catholic faith.

The first four paragraphs of that first section (CCC 1324 through CCC 1327) give us a beautiful and brief summary of the essence of the Catholic Church's belief in the Holy Eucharist. They are repeated in their entirety below.

CCC1324 - The Eucharist is "the source and summit of the Christian life". "The other sacraments, and indeed all ecclesiastical ministries and works of the apostolate, are bound up with the Eucharist and are oriented toward it. For in the Blessed Eucharist is contained the whole spiritual good of the Church, namely Christ himself, our Pasch."

CCC 1325 - "The Eucharist is the efficacious sign and sublime cause of that communion in the divine life and that unity of the People of God by which the Church is kept in being. It is the culmination, both of God's action sanctifying the world in Christ and of the worship men offer to Christ and through him to the Father in the Holy Spirit."

CCC 1326 - Finally, by the Eucharistic celebration we already unite ourselves with the heavenly liturgy and anticipate eternal life, when God will be all in all.

CCC 1327 - In brief, the Eucharist is the sum and summary of our faith: "Our way of thinking is attuned to the Eucharist, and the Eucharist in turn confirms our way of thinking."

As noted in the beginning of this chapter, the Catechism beautifully sets forth the Church's teaching of the Eucharist, which it also calls the Sacrament of Sacraments. The Sacrament very appropriately has an entire section in the Catechism and deserves greater teaching, because as St. John Paul II noted when he released it; it is the "sure norm" for teaching the Catholic faith.

It is my personal view that the section of the Catechism covering the Eucharist should be covered comprehensively for Holy Communion and Confirmation candidates as well as for candidates wishing to join the Catholic faith (RCIA classes).

Because the Catechism is the "sure norm" for teaching the Catholic faith, frequent references will be made to it is this book.

It would be too voluminous to repeat all the Catechism has to say on the beliefs of the Church, so for the remainder of this chapter we will set forth those beliefs we view as the most pertinent and descriptive messages relating to the Eucharist.

In my opinion the most evangelical words uttered by our Lord were his concluding words at the Last Supper with his Apostles on the night before He died; "Do This in Memory of Me". CCC 1341 explains his invitation to all of us as follows:

The command of Jesus to repeat his actions and words "until he comes" does not only ask us to remember Jesus and what he did. It is directed at the liturgical celebration, by the apostles and their successors, of the memorial of Christ, of his life, of his death, of his Resurrection, and of his intercession in the presence of the Father.

As noted earlier, the Church describes the Eucharist as the "Source and Summit of Ecclesial Life". It is the centerpiece of the Catholic faith. It is the primary reason that Catholics are Catholics. It is the response of the members of the Catholic faith to "Do This in Memory of Me".

CCC 1348 describes the action of Ecclesial Life as follows: *All gather together. Christians come together in one place for the Eucharistic assembly. At its head is Christ himself, the principal agent of the Eucharist. He is high priest of the New Covenant; it is he himself who presides invisibly over every Eucharistic celebration. It is in representing him that the bishop or priest acting in the person of Christ the head (in persona Christi capitis) presides over the assembly, speaks after the readings, receives the offerings, and says the Eucharistic Prayer. All have their own active parts to play in the celebration, each in his own way: readers, those who bring up the offerings, those who give communion, and the whole people whose "Amen" manifests their participation.*

In CCC 1356 the Catechism further explains the Eucharist as follows: *If from the beginning Christians have celebrated the Eucharist and in a form whose substance has not changed despite the great diversity of times and liturgies, it is because we know ourselves to be bound by the command the Lord gave on the eve of his Passion: "Do This in remembrance of me".*

To "Do This in remembrance of me" is not only a request the Lord gave us on the eve of his Passion, but an invitation to be with Him frequently through this Sacrament of Sacraments, the Holy Communion. If we flawed humans could only better understand the degree to which that invitation prepares us for eternal life with Him, we would want to share in it as often as we possibly can.

As Catholics we often refer to the reception of the Eucharist as "Holy Communion". We believe and use those words because we do believe that the Eucharist unites us more closely with the Body, Blood, Soul and Divinity of our Lord.

CCC 1392 of the Catechism describes that union in the following manner:

What material food produces in our bodily life, Holy Communion wonderfully achieves in our spiritual life. Communion with the flesh of the risen Christ, a flesh "given life and giving life through the Holy Spirit," preserves, increases, and renews the life of grace received in Baptism. This growth in Christian life needs the nourishment of Eucharistic Communion, the bread for our pilgrimage until the moment of death, when it will be given to us as viaticum.

CCC 1393 goes on to tell us more of this Holy Communion. At the end of this paragraph, the words of St. Ambrose are included parenthetically:

Holy Communion separates us from sin. The body of Christ we receive in Holy Communion is "given up for us," and the blood we drink "shed for the many for the forgiveness of sins." For this reason the Eucharist cannot unite us to Christ without at the same time preserving us from future sins: "For as often as we eat this bread and drink the cup, we proclaim the death of the Lord. If we proclaim the Lord's death, we proclaim the forgiveness of sins. If, as often as his blood is poured out, it is poured for the forgiveness of sins, I should always receive it, so that it may always forgive my sins. Because I always sin, I should always have a remedy."

As CCC 1392 states, our "growth in Christian life needs the nourishment of Eucharistic Communion". That nourishment of our soul is important to our growth in faith, spiritual wisdom and holiness. As flawed humans we cannot fully understand how this growth occurs but in faith we accept and know that it does. The mystery of our faith and the mystery of the Eucharist are intertwined in this Sacrament of Sacraments. We need the frequent reception of the Eucharist to more closely align ourselves with the "things of God". It helps us break our attachment to the mammon of this world.

CCC 1419 concludes the section on the Eucharist in the Catechism and further explains how the Eucharist aligns us with the "things of God".

Having passed from this world to the Father, Christ gives us in the Eucharist the pledge of glory with him. Participation in the Holy Sacrifice identifies us with his Heart, sustains our strength along the pilgrimage of this life, makes us long for eternal life, and unites us even now to the Church in heaven, the Blessed Virgin Mary, and all the saints.

CHAPTER 3

EARLY CHURCH HISTORY

Following the Ascension of Jesus and the Descent of the Holy Spirit, the Apostles often gathered together to celebrate Mass and the Eucharist. Sacred Scripture in the Acts of the Apostles records such events

In Chapter 2 of the Acts of the Apostles and following Pentecost, Peter began preaching in Jerusalem and there were many who were baptized. Following those conversions, Chapter 2 of the Acts of the Apostles tells us of their dedication to the Eucharist as follows:

Communal Life *- They devoted themselves to the teaching of the apostles and to the communal life, to the breaking of the bread and to the prayers. Awe came upon everyone, and many wonders and signs were done through the apostles. All who believed were together and had all things in common; they would sell their property and possessions and divide* *them among all according to each one's need. Every day they devoted themselves to meeting together in the temple area and to breaking bread in their homes. They ate their meals with exultation and sincerity of heart, praising God and enjoying favor with all the people. And every day the Lord added to their number those who were being saved.*

It is noteworthy to reflect on the words, "Awe came upon everyone". The title of this book is "The Miracle of the Eucharist". One of those miracles is the supernatural impact the "breaking of the bread" has on the human and invisible soul. "Awe" comes upon those who partake in ways we cannot fully comprehend. We can only believe that the Eucharist provides that nourishment of the soul to produce the "awe" of increased faith and spiritual wisdom together with greater insights into the Kingdom He opened.

The Eucharist was also noted several times later in the Acts. These notations were related to St. Paul. In Acts Chapter 20, in his journey to Troas, the following is noted:

On the first day of the week when we gathered to break bread, Paul spoke to them because he was going to leave on the next day, and he kept on speaking until midnight. There were many lamps in the upstairs room where we were gathered, and a young man named Eutychus who was sitting on the window sill was sinking into a deep sleep as Paul talked on and on. Once overcome by sleep, he fell down from the third story and when he was picked up, he was dead.

Paul went down, threw himself upon him, and said as he embraced him, "Don't be alarmed; there is life in him." Then he returned upstairs, broke the bread, and ate; after a long conversation that lasted until daybreak, he departed. And they took the boy away alive and were immeasurably comforted.

In the above instance, and in many others, the breaking of the bread was accompanied by marvelous deeds. In Chapter 1 we noted how the disciples, who walked with Jesus on the road to Emmaus had their eyes opened upon the breaking of the bread by Jesus. As implied in Chapter 2 of Acts, "breaking of the bread" seemed to be accompanied by the conversion of many to become believers and "were being saved".

At the time of early Christianity it was a common practice that the Eucharist was celebrated in the homes of those who were believers. The numbers of those who became Christians also increased rapidly during that period of early Christianity. The Eucharist has a long history of being the cornerstone of evangelization. A later chapter will explore that in greater detail.

Even though the celebration of the Mass has changed over the past two thousand years, the one constant has been that the Eucharist has always been the core of the liturgy. In the next chapter we will explore in greater detail the dedication of early saints to the Eucharist. Their descriptions of the celebration of the Eucharist, especially that of St. Justin, provide insights as to how the Mass developed in those early stages of Christianity.

The early Mass developed gradually. The breaking of the bread included rituals from the Jewish celebrations in their synagogues. Readings were taken from the Old Testament as well as from the scriptures which would become the New Testament. Such readings would include the letters and testimonies of the apostles and early disciples. Psalms were sung as is often done today. The core elements of the Liturgy of the Word and the Liturgy of the Eucharist as we know it today found its roots in those early celebrations of the Eucharist.

During the early Church there were many persecutions against Christians. The celebrations of the Eucharist could not always take place openly. The celebrations would be held often secretly in homes or other places. Among those were the early catacombs. While the catacombs were useful for other purposes, especially burials, they were also places of worship.

Early Christians suffered many hardships in the pursuit of their Christian faith. With the exception of John, the other Apostles were martyred. That was also true of many of our early saints and many others who were faithful to our Lord.

The title of this book, "The Miracle of the Eucharist" was not only chosen because of the transformation of bread and wine into the Body, Blood, Soul and Divinity of our Lord, but also because of its invisible but nevertheless miraculous effect on those who believe. That belief is very powerful and many have been willing to sacrifice their lives for it. In those faithful souls the strength of the soul overcomes the weakness of the flesh.

The power of faith has a miraculous impact on believers. At the core of their belief is the Eucharist which is so deeply entrenched in their soul that it overcomes all fear of things of earth. Although God's creation should lead all humans to a belief in a Divine Creator, things of the world cannot alone lead to an increase in faith. But the faith of those who fervently partake in the breaking of the bread does increase as does spiritual wisdom and holiness.

The Eucharist from early Christianity until today is the ultimate expression of love Christians display for He who died for them. From the earliest of Christians came the belief that "unless you eat of my flesh and drink of my blood, you cannot have life within you". That life within us is the ultimate way we have to show our love of Him who came to earth to suffer and die for us so we can spend eternity with Him.

When our Lord spoke of the "life within you", He was speaking of the divinity that He was sharing with our soul. Therein is the miracle of the Eucharist for those who believe and partake in the breaking of the bread. The divinity that we share with Him when we partake is not a natural phenomenon but rather a supernatural sharing with our Lord. It is indeed a miracle for our soul.

That belief and that love of the Eucharist goes beyond the love we understand associated with things on earth. When the early Christians as well as Christians of today are willing to sacrifice their life on earth for their love of Him, they are practicing a love that more closely resembles the Divine Love our Lord demonstrated in his death on the Cross. It indeed has its divine and miraculous aspects because it cannot be explained in human terms.

It is worthwhile for all Christians to study the sacrifice and love of the Apostles and early saints for Him who died for them. They serve as models for all of us to emulate.

Many of the early disciples abandoned Jesus following his Discourse on the Bread of Life. They simply found it too "hard" to believe. Throughout the history of the Church many others have found it too "hard" to believe. The Eucharist is a measurement of the depth of faith. Why some believe whereas others do not is a mystery. Such it was at the time of our Lord and such it is today.

One of the trademarks of saints is their deep dedication to the Holy Eucharist. That was true in the early stages of the Church and remains true today. The dedication of a number of such saints will be addressed in the next chapter.

CHAPTER 4

EUCHARISTIC TESTIMONIES OF SAINTS

As was noted at the end of the last chapter, our saints had a deep devotion to the Holy Eucharist.

One of the earliest examples we have of such a saint is St. Justin Martyr, who was born near the beginning of the 2nd century. In his First Apology (a defense of Christianity) to the Roman Emperor and others he gave one of the best descriptions of how and why early Christians came together to celebrate the Mass and Eucharist. In CCC 1345 our Catechism provides us with those words as follows:

On the day we call the day of the sun, all who dwell in the city or country gather in the same place.

The memoirs of the apostles and the writings of the prophets are read, as much as time permits.

When the reader has finished, he who presides over those gathered admonishes and challenges them to imitate these beautiful things.

Then we all rise together and offer prayers for ourselves... and for all others, wherever they may be, so that we may be found righteous by our life and actions, and faithful to the commandments, so as to obtain eternal salvation.

When the prayers are concluded we exchange the kiss.

Then someone brings bread and a cup of water and wine mixed together to him who presides over the brethren.

He takes them and offers praise and glory to the Father of the universe, through the name of the Son and of the Holy Spirit and for a considerable time he gives thanks (in Greek: eucharistian) that we have been judged worthy of these gifts.

When he has concluded the prayers and thanksgivings, all present give voice to an acclamation by saying: 'Amen.'

When he who presides has given thanks and the people have responded, those whom we call deacons give to those present the "eucharisted" bread, wine and water and take them to those who are absent.

Much of the descriptions by St. Justin are akin to the Mass of modern times. St. Justin goes on in the First Apology to more fully describe the Eucharist.

And this food is called among us the Eucharist, of which no one is allowed to partake but the man who believes that the things which we teach are true, and who has been washed with the washing that is for the remission of sins, and unto regeneration, and who is so living as Christ has enjoined.

For not as common bread and common drink do we receive these; but in like manner as Jesus Christ our Savior, having been made flesh by the Word of God, had both flesh and blood for our salvation, so likewise have we been taught that the food is blessed by the prayer of his word, and from which our blood and flesh by transmutation are nourished, is the flesh and blood of that Jesus who was made flesh.

The description of the Eucharist by St. Justin was essentially the same as was confirmed by the Council of Trent fourteen hundred years later and the same as we believe to this day. In 165 A.D. St. Justin was martyred for his beliefs and for his refusal to offer sacrifices to the Roman gods.

In addition to St. Justin, numerous other saints have expressed their deep reverence and dedication to the Eucharist. We will add a few of the more prominent testimonies in this chapter.

St. Irenaeus, who was the second bishop of Lyons, was another early pillar and saint of our Church. In his writings, which also took place in the latter 2nd century, He stated the following in regards to the Eucharist:

So then, if the mixed cup and the manufactured bread receive the Word of God and become the Eucharist, that is to say, the Blood and Body of Christ, which fortify and build up the substance of our flesh, how can people claim that the flesh is incapable of receiving God's gift of eternal life, when it is nourished by Christ's Blood and Body and is His member? As the blessed apostle says in his letter to the Ephesians, 'For we are members of His Body, of His flesh and of His bones'."

In the same writing St. Irenaeus states the following in regard to the transubstantiation of the Bread and Wine. *These two then receive the Word of God and become the Eucharist, which is the Body and Blood of Christ.*

We add the words of St. Irenaeus, to further fortify the belief of the Church from its earliest days, that the transubstantiation of bread and wine into the Body and Blood of Christ has been in existence since the beginning of our Church.

St. Jerome, another saint of the Church commented as follows in regards to the Eucharist:

If Christ did not want to dismiss the Jews without food in the desert for fear that they would collapse on the way, it was to teach us that it is dangerous to try to get to heaven without the Bread of Heaven.

It is not only the belief in the miracle of the Eucharist that is a trademark of our saints, but it is the love of our Lord through the Eucharist which many of our saints so dearly cherished. From the saints of the early Church we will now note some of the views of more modern day saints.

One of my favorites and very short statements of the Eucharist was made by St. Maximilian Kolbe as follows: *The culmination of the Mass is not the consecration, but Communion.*

It is one of my favorites because St. Maximilian seems to be saying that the highest point of the Mass is the miracle of our Holy Communion rather than the miracle of transubstantiation. That also implies that those who receive Communion share in a very special and divine way, the Body, Blood, Soul and Divinity of our Lord. Because of the importance of that divinity to our soul, the next chapter of this book will cover the divine aspects of the Eucharist.

St. Maximilian provided another brief statement on the Eucharist which is worth noting. *If angels could be jealous of men, they would be so for one reason: Holy Communion.*

A great saint of the 19th century, St. Peter Julian Eymard, was especially devoted to the Eucharist. He was born in the French Alps in 1811. Early in his priestly life, he experienced a spiritual encounter with our Lord, which gave him a lifelong love of the goodness of our Lord. Some of his views regarding the Eucharist indicate the great love affair he had with the Lord.

Love cannot triumph unless it becomes the one passion of our life. Without such passions we may produce isolated acts of love; but our life is not really won over or consecrated to an ideal. He went on to add: *Until we have a passionate love for our Lord in the Most Blessed Sacrament we shall accomplish nothing.*

St. Peter Julian urged all the faithful to participate in the Eucharist on a daily basis. He believed that the Eucharist provided a special grace. That special grace comes to us in our divine sharing of His Body, Blood, Soul and Divinity. St. Peter Julian throughout his life, had a special dedication to the Sacrament of Divine Love.

We will bring this chapter to a close with a number of testimonies to the Blessed Sacrament from saints as compiled by the "Real Presence Eucharistic and Adoration Association".

St. Francis de Sales - *When you have received Him, stir up your heart to do Him homage; speak to Him about your spiritual life, gazing upon Him in your soul where He is present for your happiness; welcome Him as warmly as possible, and behave outwardly in such a way that your actions may give proof to all of His presence.*

St. John Vianney - *All the good works in the world are not equal to the Holy Sacrifice of the Mass because they are the works of men; but the Mass is the work of God. Martyrdom is nothing in comparison, for it is but the sacrifice of man to God: but the mass is the sacrifice of God for man.*

St. Therese of Lisieux - *It is not to remain in a golden ciborium that He comes down to each from Heaven, but to find another Heaven, the Heaven of our soul in which He takes delight.*

St. Damien, Apostle of Lepers - *The Blessed Sacrament is indeed the stimulus for us all, for me as it should be for you, to forsake all worldly ambitions. Without the constant presence of our Divine Master upon the altar in my poor chapels, I never could have persevered casting my lot with the lepers of Molokai the foreseen consequence of which begins now to appear on my skin, and is felt throughout the body. Holy Communion being the daily bread of a priest, I feel myself happy, well pleased, and resigned in the rather exceptional circumstances in which it has pleased Divine Providence to put me.*

This chapter of the book was added because it provides the testimony of saints that the Holy Eucharist is the ultimate requirement to greater faith, greater spiritual wisdom and greater holiness. It is the Sacrament of Sacraments and it is the Sacrament of Divine Love.

CHAPTER 5

THE DIVINE ASPECTS
OF THE EUCHARIST

Through the Eucharist, humanity and divinity are linked. It is an unfortunate truth that within our Catholic Church the divine aspects of the Eucharist are not frequently addressed. The Catechism does a wonderful job on fully explaining the Eucharist but those teachings are poorly communicated. That is somewhat understandable as to the divine aspects, because so much of what we believe of divinity relates to the individualistic perceptions attributable to our faith. And because we are flawed humans, our personal perceptions of divinity are also flawed to some degree, and thus the understandable humility and timidity in stating those views.

St. Peter Julian Eymard was a notable exception to the aforementioned lack of teaching on the divine aspects of the Eucharist. Among his many comments on the Eucharist, some of which were noted in the prior chapter, the following is especially noteworthy: *Do you wish to learn the secret of true Eucharistic prayer? Consider, then, all the mysteries in the light of the Blessed Sacrament. It is a divine prism through which they can all be studied.*

The saint also noted that: *The Eucharist is, in a word, the great Mystery of our faith to which all Catholic truths lead.* The saint is essentially telling us that if we wish to increase our understanding of divinity, such understanding can best be achieved through the Eucharist.

Because the Eucharist is the great Mystery of our faith, it is difficult to speak or write much on the subject of that Mystery and it is probably a major reason that the mystical and divine aspects of the Eucharist are given such little attention. Nevertheless, the divine aspects deserve greater attention from all of us. But as is true with all mysteries, earthly proof of many of such divine aspects does not exist.

It is not always easy to remember, as a part of the Holy Eucharist, that our Lord has both a human and divine nature and that it is impossible, as the Council of Chalcedon taught us, when speaking of our Lord, to address his two natures separately. Too often, such attempts are made. Nevertheless, our Lord was true God and true man and thus the Eucharist is not only the Body and Blood of our Lord, but also the Soul and Divinity.

It is good for us to remember that the Jesus, who was born in a stable, who walked on water, who rose Lazarus from the dead and who suffered and died for our sins, is the same Jesus of the Holy Eucharist. When receiving Holy Communion it is also the same Jesus, who becomes nourishment for our soul. That impact on our soul is among the aforementioned mysteries, and much of it is shrouded in divinity.

The Catechism in its descriptions of the Eucharist touches on the divine and mysterious aspects in the following manner:

The Holy and <u>Divine</u> Liturgy, because the Church's whole liturgy finds its center and most intense expression in the celebration of this sacrament; in the same sense we also call its celebration the Sacred Mysteries. We speak of the Most Blessed Sacrament because it is the Sacrament of Sacraments. The Eucharistic species reserved in the tabernacle are designated by the same name.

As urged earlier in this book, an entire reading of Article 3 in the Catechism will provide a helpful and wonderful insight into the Eucharist.

Because the Eucharist is the Sacrament of Sacraments, we need to make that more broadly known. Studies and polls show that of those baptized into the Catholic faith, only about twenty percent practice their faith by the time they graduate from college. It is my unwavering belief, that if all aspects of the Eucharist are more broadly taught and acknowledged to be the Sacrament of Sacraments, more members of our younger generation would practice their faith.

This book addresses the Eucharist as a miracle and that it is when the bread and wine are transubstantiated into the Body, Blood, Soul and Divinity of our Lord.

But the miracle of the Eucharist extends beyond the transubstantiation. It is a miracle with divine aspects in the many ways it transforms our soul. When we humbly and devotedly receive Holy Communion we partake in the Real Presence and that extends to the divine nature of our Lord.

When we partake in that Holy Communion we become more Godlike because God has become a part of us. Therein lies the great and divine mystical aspects for humans of the Sacrament of Sacraments - that God would humble Himself to permit us to share, albeit ever so slightly, in his Divinity. This He does because of his love for us, despite our sinful nature.

When we frequently and fervently receive Holy Communion, we become more closely and divinely aligned to Him who asked that we "Do This in remembrance of Me". As we become more divinely aligned with Him, we begin seeing more and more things through the divine prism of which St. Peter Julian Eymard spoke.

Through the reception of Holy Communion, we will come to appreciate and give thanks to God the Father for all his wondrous creation. We will be ever closer to our Lord Jesus, who suffered and died for us and we will grow in faith and spiritual wisdom as we better comprehend the spiritual guidance of the Holy Spirit.

At the beginning of this chapter we bemoaned the lack of attention given to the Eucharist, because of the lack of catechetical and other verbal teachings, but as also noted, the Catechism of the Catholic Church is comprehensive in the beauties of the Eucharist and makes note of the spiritual benefits to be derived from it. We will note a few of those.

CCC 1358 makes note of the considerations we make of the Eucharist:
- *thanksgiving and praise to the Father*
- *the sacrificial memorial of Christ and his Body;*
- *the presence of Christ by the power of his word and of his Spirit.*

In CCC 1359 through 1361 the Catechism notes the thanksgiving and praise to the Father, which should be attributable to the Eucharist.

CCC 1359 - *The Eucharist, the sacrament of our salvation accomplished by Christ on the cross, is also a sacrifice of praise in thanksgiving for the work of creation. In the Eucharistic sacrifice the whole of creation loved by God is presented to* the Father through the death and the Resurrection of Christ. Through Christ, the Church can offer the sacrifice of praise in thanksgiving for all that God has made good, beautiful and just in creation and in humanity.

CCC 1360 - *The Eucharist is a sacrifice of thanksgiving to the Father, a blessing by which the Church expresses her gratitude to God for all his benefits, for all that he has accomplished through creation, redemption, and sanctification. Eucharist means first of all "thanksgiving"*

CCC 1361 - *The Eucharist is also the sacrifice of praise by which the Church sings the glory of God in the name of all creation. This sacrifice of praise is possible only through Christ: he unites the faithful to his person, to his praise, and to his intercession, so that the sacrifice of praise to the Father is offered through Christ and with him, to be accepted in him.*

The Catechism in CCC 1362 through 1372 addresses the sacrificial memorial of Christ and of his Body, the Church. Much of what is contained in those paragraphs is referenced elsewhere in this book.

Our Catechism also speaks to "The Presence of Christ by the power of his word and the Holy Spirit". It is not the Catechism that is lacking in expressing the beauty of the Eucharist, but rather the attention in teaching that which is contained in the Catechism.

The Sacrament of Sacraments is not a Sacrament that can be fully understood or appreciated by our human senses. It is through our faith and spiritual wisdom that we understand and appreciate the divine nature of Holy Communion. Our Holy Communion with Him is the best way we have on earth to increase our faith, spiritual wisdom and holiness. That is part of the beautiful, mysterious, and divine aspects of the Eucharist.

The Church has many different names by which it addresses the Eucharist. They include;

The Lord's Supper
The Breading of the Bread
The Eucharistic Assembly
The Memorial of the Lord's Passion and Resurrection
The Holy Sacrifice (Holy Sacrifice of
the Mass, Sacrifice of Praise, and
Spiritual Sacrifice are also used)
The Holy and Divine Liturgy
Holy Communion
Holy Mass

All of the aforementioned are apt descriptions of the Eucharist. My personal favorite has become the "Sacrament of Divine Love". I like that description because (for me) it conveys the message that the Eucharist is a Holy Communion with He who is both Divine and Love.

The Sacrament of Divine Love is also a wonderful description because in receiving Holy Communion we humans "share" in our Lord's divinity. But in the flawed nature of humans we return to sin. And in his Divine Love he again forgives and through his divine mercy He again heals our soul.

Through frequent reception of Holy Communion, we can more fully align our soul with our Savior. The disruptions of things on earth diminish and the "things of God" are raised to a higher level. The more frequently we participate in the Eucharist, the more clearly we understand his divine majesty, through the beauty and wonders of his creation, and the great love extended to us through his salvation. And we will also have a greater appreciation and awareness of the guidance of the Holy Spirit.

Holy Communion, in a mysterious and divine manner, helps humans to better comprehend the beauties of his divinity. Therein lies another miracle of the Eucharist, because it is not our human senses that comprehend the wondrous beauty of his divinity, but rather the spiritual wisdom of our soul.

It is unfortunate that as humans we are not capable of comprehending all of the many divine aspects of the Eucharist. But they are reasons for us to meditate on them and with the help of Holy Communion we are better able to understand.

It is acknowledged by our Church, and a teaching of our Church, that frequent and fervent reception of Holy Communion results in humans growing in love and holiness. The Church and Scripture also acknowledge that our Lord is Love. As our love of Him increases, it may also be that we partake in his love and divinity in ways we do not understand.

It may also be that in ways we humans cannot fully comprehend, the Eucharist helps us grow in faith, spiritual wisdom and holiness, because it is the apex of our faith.

Is it really a result of the divine aspects of the Eucharist that humans grow in love, holiness, faith and spiritual wisdom? In my opinion the answer to that question must be yes because we share in his Body, Blood, Soul and Divinity. But because divinity is shrouded in mystery we cannot fully understand the complete role the Eucharist plays in the divine effects it has on humans.

CHAPTER 6

EUCHARISTIC ADORATION

In my parish, we have the Exposition of the Blessed Sacrament every Thursday morning following our 8:00 am Mass. The Eucharist remains exposed until noon. My hour with our Lord during that period of time is one of the best hours I spend each week. Associated with some chores I do for our parish, it is also possible for me to spend about a half hour each morning in our Adoration Chapel.

Because of the mystery of faith, we cannot explain in words the joy that comes with spending Adoration time with our Lord. It permits us time to marvel at the majesty and beauty of creation, the great love demonstrated for our personal salvation through the passion, death and resurrection of our Lord and it helps increase our understanding of the spiritual guidance provided by the Holy Spirit.

We also refer to the Exposition of the Blessed Sacrament as the Adoration of the Blessed Sacrament. It is that Adoration which makes the time spent with him so very special.

It is his first command that we love Him with all our heart, soul, mind and strength. Next to receiving Holy Communion there is no better way for us to observe his command than through the Adoration of the Blessed Sacrament. Through that Adoration his command becomes our greatest joy.

Through Adoration we find it easier to set aside our own sinful pride. By doing that we are more able to focus our heart, soul and mind on adoring Him with whom we wish to spend eternal life. If we wish to spend eternity in his presence, visits to the Blessed Sacrament are a wonderful precursor to that eternal life.

Adoration time with Him who wrought our salvation is not only a precursor to eternal life, it fills us with a greater desire for that eternal life with Him.

In chapter four we noted that many of our great saints had a special dedication to the Holy Eucharist. Such dedication by our saints extends to their time spent with our Lord in Adoration and many have also given their testimony to that joyful experience.

St. Alphonsus Liguori wrote: *Of all the devotions, that of adoring Jesus in the Blessed Sacrament is the greatest after the sacraments, the one dearest to God and the most helpful to us.*

St. Alphonsus went on to state: *Do not then, O devout soul, refuse to begin this devotion; and forsaking the conversation of men, dwell each day, from this time forward, for at least half or quarter of an hour in some church in the presence of Jesus Christ under the sacramental species...Be assured that the time you will thus spend with devotion before this most divine Sacrament will be the most profitable to you in your life and the source of your greatest consolation in death and eternity. You must also be aware that in a quarter of an hour's prayer spent in the presence of the Blessed Sacrament, you will perhaps gain more than in all the other spiritual exercises of the day.*

St. Maria Faustina Kowalska, the "Apostle of The Divine Mercy" is considered one of the outstanding mystics of our Church. It was to St. Faustina, that our Lord provided the words of the Divine Mercy chaplet, which is so often prayed during periods of Adoration.

St. Faustina's Diary is a beautiful tribute to our Lord's Divine Mercy. In her Diary she gives us some of the divine benefits of the Blessed Sacrament.

I adore you, Lord and Creator, hidden in the Most Blessed Sacrament, I adore You for all the works of Your hands, that reveal to me so much wisdom, goodness, and mercy, O Lord.

You have spread so much beauty over the earth and it tells me about Your beauty, even though these beautiful things are but a faint reflection of You (who is) incomprehensible Beauty. And although You have hidden Yourself and concealed your beauty, my eye, enlightened by faith, reaches You and my soul recognizes its Creator, its Highest Good, and my heart is completely immersed in prayer of adoration.

As noted elsewhere in this book, the human language is not adequate for expressing the divine aspects and benefits of the Eucharist, but St. Faustina comes as close as one can to doing that in her Diary. When the eyes of our soul are more "enlightened by faith" we come closer and closer to better appreciating that day when we will spend eternity in his presence.

Elsewhere in her Diary, St. Faustina goes on to state the following:

To converse with You, O Lord, is the delight of my heart. In You I find everything that my heart could desire. Here Your light illumines my mind, enabling it to know You more and more deeply.

St. Faustina wished to share her mystical experiences with the entire world. She longed to have all people delight in his love and share more greatly in his Divine Mercy. It is through the Adoration of the Blessed Sacrament that we can move closer to the joys expressed by St. Faustina.

Through our Adoration of the Blessed Sacrament, we can acknowledge our Lord in numerous ways. We can use our Adoration time for devotions to his Sacred Heart and also to his Divine Mercy. Through Adoration we put into action those words of the Gloria. *We praise you, we bless you, we adore you, we give you thanks for your great glory, Lord God, heavenly King, O God almighty Father.*

St. John Paul II had a deep and fervent dedication to the Holy Eucharist and to the Adoration of the Blessed Sacrament. He spoke often of The Sacrament of Divine Love. We will close this chapter with the words he spoke when inaugurating Perpetual Adoration at St. Peter's at the beginning of Advent in 1981.

LORD STAY WITH US - These words were spoken for the first time by the disciples of Emmaus. Subsequently in the course of the centuries they have been spoken an infinite number of times, by the lips of so many of Your disciples and confessors, O Christ.

STAY WITH US TODAY and stay, from now on, every day, according to the desire of my heart, which accepts the appeal of so many hearts from various parts, sometimes far away, and above all meets the desire of so many inhabitants of the Apostolic See.

STAY! That we may meet You in the prayer of adoration and thanksgiving, in the prayer of expiation and petition, to which all those who visit this basilica are invited. Stay! You

Who are at one and the same time veiled in the Eucharistic Mystery of Faith and are also revealed under the species of bread and wine, which You have assumed in this Sacrament.

Stay! That your presence in this temple may incessantly be reconfirmed, and that all those who enter here may become aware that it is your house, "the dwelling of God with men" and visiting this basilica, may find in it the very source of life and holiness that gushes forth from your Eucharistic heart...

One day, oh Lord, You asked Peter: "Do you love Me?" You asked him three times - and three times the Apostle answered: "Lord You know everything, You know that I love You." May the answer of Peter, on whose tomb this basilica was erected, be expressed by this daily and day-long adoration which we have begun today.

Wherever in this world the Adoration of the Blessed Sacrament takes place, the opportunity to respond to Our Lord's question, "Do you love Me". is made available to all of us. In every Adoration of this Blessed Sacrament we can answer Him who is exposed in the monstrance "Lord You know that I love you".

CHAPTER 7

THE CORNERSTONE OF EVANGELIZATION

During the past sixty years, there has been a substantial and steady decline of participation by Catholics in their faith. During that period there has also been a decline in the use of standard catechetical teaching of the Catholic faith.

Recently I received correspondence from the Sophia Institute, which was organized to train teachers of the Catholic faith. In that correspondence reference was made to a survey of Catholic religion teachers. One of the findings of the survey was that fully half of the Catholic religion teachers had either not attended a Catholic high school or had received no Catholic schooling at all.

Prior to the 1960's there was a significant number of religious, who were teaching religion to Catholic children. Also prior to the 1960's there was considerable usage of the Baltimore Catechism for teaching the Catholic faith to our youth.

The reduced use of the Baltimore Catechism combined with the reduction in the number of religious personnel teaching religion has led to an increase in the diversity of teaching the Catholic faith. Those changes during the past sixty years have impacted the teaching of the significant role that the Eucharist has in the Catholic faith.

In mid-2017 an article, "Eucharist - The Cornerstone of Evangelization" was written by me and published by several diocesan newspapers. That article is reproduced in its entirety below.

God is not dead, but too often we treat Him that way.

One must wait until Page 334 in the Catechism of the Catholic Church before one finds coverage of The Sacrament of the Eucharist. But once found, we see it covered as the "Source and Summit of Ecclesial Life". Later, on that same page, in CCC 1327 we are told that "In brief, the Eucharist is the sum and summary of our faith".

The Vatican II Council made a number of references to the importance of the Eucharist to evangelization. Among the more important ones are the following: "The most blessed Eucharist contains the Church's entire spiritual wealth" and

"The Eucharist shows itself to be the source and apex of the whole proclamation of the Gospel".

On the night before our Lord endured the Passion and suffered Crucifixion on the Cross, He instituted the Eucharist at the Last Supper and concluded with the words. "Do This in Memory of Me". His suffering, death and resurrection formed his part of the new covenant He gave us. Our part of the covenant is to keep his commandments and to remember his suffering and passion through the Eucharist. In the Eucharist we commemorate the death on the cross endured by Him and through which He redeemed our sins and earned for us the opportunity to spend eternal life in the Kingdom He opened for us. It is indeed the sum and summary of our faith.

If the Eucharist "contains the Church's entire spiritual wealth" it is fair to ask why it is not given earlier coverage in the Catechism and why it still gets too little attention. The answer is somewhat reflective of the unintended consequences of Vatican II. As noted earlier, Vatican II did not diminish the role of the Eucharist in the "proclamation of the Gospel". However, Vatican II did focus on other matters, and in the greater attention given to those matters, which were important, the "apex of the whole proclamation of the Gospel" too frequently lost top billing.

In the period of time since Vatican II, Mass attendance among Catholics has declined from approximately fifty percent to about twenty percent. If we wish to reverse that trend we must again firmly establish the Eucharist as the cornerstone of evangelization and make that better known to those who do not find relevancy in attending Mass. If all of us do a better job of conveying the message of the miracle of the Eucharist, Mass attendance will increase.

In the article, the unintended consequences of Vatican II's affect on the Eucharist is noted. In no way is that notation intended to diminish the very important contributions of that Council. But as also noted, those contributions, to some degree, transferred the focus and importance of the Eucharist to other important, but nevertheless, less important matters.

As previously noted in this book, St. John Vianney believed and proclaimed that the Eucharist is superior to all the good works of humans, because the Eucharist is the work of God, whereas good works are the work of humans. As noted earlier that does not diminish the good works of humans, but the work and things of God must always be considered as the apex of our faith.

If we are to increase the participation of Catholics in their faith, we must increase the importance that the Eucharist has to our Catholic faith. The Catechism properly refers to the Eucharist as the "sum and summary of our faith" It is long overdue that the Eucharist be treated that way in both word and action.

When we speak of the Catholic faith without speaking of the Eucharist, we miss "the entire spiritual wealth" of

Catholicism. If we truly believe that the Eucharist is the "sum and summary of our faith", how can it not play a substantial role in our catholic faith discussions.

God is love and makes Himself present to us in the Eucharist. To partake in the Mass and the Eucharist is to embrace his love. It is the Sacrament of Sacraments and the Sacrament of Divine Love. It needs to be proclaimed as such.

In the Sacrament of Divine Love we become united with God's love. Through the mysterious miracle of the Sacrament we grow in faith, spiritual wisdom and holiness.

Our Lord reminded us that unless we eat of his flesh and drink of his blood we will not have LIFE within us. In that reference he speaks to the LIFE of our soul and that we need to partake in Holy Communion to have such LIFE.

He went on to say that it is the spirit (soul) which gives LIFE and that the flesh is of no avail. It is the Eucharist which nourishes the soul and because of that nourishment our soul is able to grow in faith and spiritual wisdom. Through that nourishment of the soul, we receive the gift that sustains us spiritually in this life and into eternity.

The Eucharist must be firmly established and proclaimed as the cornerstone of evangelization if we wish to increase participation in our Catholic faith. In doing that we need not diminish our good works. Our Lord told us if we have faith in Him we will do good works and there is no greater way to demonstrate our faith than to receive Him in Holy Communion.

We must proclaim to all who don't know or who doubt, that through the Eucharist we have the opportunity to demonstrate our love for Him. In doing that we also obey his first commandment that we love Him with our all heart, soul, mind and strength. We will not only obey that commandment, but will learn to love it.

Finally, we must convey the message that in receiving Holy Communion we are fulfilling his invitation to "Do This in Memory of Me".

The Eucharist IS the cornerstone of evangelization.

CHAPTER 8

"DO THIS IN MEMORY OF ME"

On the Holy Thursday night before He died our Lord presided at the first Mass and first transubstantiation of bread and wine into His Body, Blood, Soul and Divinity. As he concluded he said the words, which are still used at the conclusion of the Consecration; "Do This in Memory of Me". With those words of Love he beckons all people on earth to remember, through the reception of Holy Communion, everything He did and does because of his great love for us.

Earlier in this book we used the words of St. John Vianney to describe his view on the importance of the Mass and Eucharist. They are worth repeating here: *All the good works in the world are not equal to the Holy Sacrifice of the Mass because they are works of men; but the Mass is the*

*work of God. Martyrdom is nothing in comparison for it is
but the sacrifice of man to God: but the Mass is the sacrifice
of God for man.*

The words of St. John Vianney express the proper view
that all people on earth should have of the Eucharist. He
came to earth to suffer and die for us so we might have
the opportunity of spending our eternal life with Him.
He told us that no greater love can be demonstrated than
to lay down one's life for another. Our Divine Savior did
that for us through his human death on the cross. On
the night before He died for us, He asked that we receive
the Holy Eucharist in memory of that passion, death and
resurrection along with everything else He does for us.

There is no greater way to express our love of Him than
through the reception of Holy Communion. It is our
frequent opportunity to unite ourselves with Him who is
Divine Love. To ignore that Divine love is to spurn Him
who wrought our salvation and made it possible for us to
spend eternity with Him.

St. John Vianney reminded us that all the good works of
men do not equal the Holy Sacrifice of the Mass and the
Eucharist. It is an unfortunate truth that in recent years
we have too often reversed those words of St. John. Our
Lord himself reminded us that if we have faith in him we
will know the good works we must do.

By placing the Holy Eucharist as the first priority of our Love of Him, we do not diminish the value of good works. But we do place the value of the Eucharist at "the sum and summary of our faith" as our Church does. Unfortunately that priority is not taught today as it needs to be. If we did nothing but teach the Eucharist as our Sacrament of Divine Love, our teaching would be adequate, because through the Eucharist we would understand the good works we need to do.

When we attend Mass and partake of the Holy Eucharist, we become a better human being, because we have shared in his Divine Love. Through Holy Communion we build a better and greater understanding within our soul of divinity and thereby are better able to work with God to build a better world through that understanding which is Love. We will shed our attachment to the things of this world because we will have a better understanding of the things of God and that the things of God lead us to a greater lasting joy in this world and the next.

It is through "Do This in Memory of Me" that we gain a better understanding of eternal life, because it is through the Eucharist that we unite heaven and earth. It is through the Eucharist that the God of Heaven humbles himself to share his divinity with the humans on earth.

It is through the Eucharist that our soul gains greater spiritual wisdom and thereby builds our understanding of the things of God noted earlier. In that process we will better appreciate the works of God. We will see more clearly the beauty and majesty of creation, have a deeper appreciation of the love that earned our salvation and a greater understanding of the spiritual guidance of the Holy Spirit.

The reception of Holy Communion is the highest form of obedience to our faith. In receiving Holy Communion we respond directly to his invitation to "Do This in Memory of Me". In doing that we build our anticipatory joy of spending eternity with Him who died for us.

We have noted several times that there has been a significant decline in the number of Catholics, who participate in the practice of their faith once they become adults. It is my conviction that it will take a better understanding through better teaching which will begin to reverse that situation. It is my belief that if the great love of our Savior is better made known, there will be a greater return of that love by those who don't understand that we can best respond to his invitation by receiving Holy Communion in memory of Him.

Pope St. John Paul II addressed the need to make our Savior better known with the following words:

I urge priests, religious and lay people to continue and redouble their efforts to teach the younger generations the meaning and value of Eucharistic adoration and devotion.

How will young people be able to know the Lord if they are not introduced to the mystery of his presence?

Unfortunately that teaching has not and is not taking place as it needs to be done. Such teaching is crucial to increasing the participation of younger generations in their faith. If the great love our Lord extends to all of us is not taught as urged by St. John Paul II, then it makes it less likely that our younger generations will reciprocate that love through Eucharist reception, adoration and devotion. The lack of teaching is depriving our youth of that greater joy which comes from the better understanding of the Eucharist.

"Do This in Memory of Me" are not just words that are repeated at every Mass at the conclusion of the Consecration. They are the words of our Lord asking us to remember Him in the most special way possible. To spurn that invitation is to spurn the love He demonstrated for each of us by humbling himself and assuming a human nature. Through that human nature He suffered and died for each of us so it would be possible to spend eternity with Him.

In the previous chapter of this book we note that the Eucharist must be the cornerstone of evangelization. It seems to me that St. John Vianney was saying the same thing when he said that all the good works of men are not equal to the Holy Sacrifice of the Mass. If we want greater participation by the younger generations in their Catholic faith. we must place the Eucharist in the place it deserves, which is at the apex of our Catholic faith.

When we present the Eucharist as the sum and summit of Ecclesial Life we must emphasize that it is the Sacrament of Divine Love. In recent years we have spoken and taught too little of the Love that is expressed in our Lord's words to "Do This in Memory of Me".

CHAPTER 9

THE NEED TO INCREASE SIGNIFICANCE OF THE EUCHARIST

In the opinion of this writer and as noted several times in this book, the greatest obstacle to increasing participation in Catholic faith is a lack of understanding in the Miracle of the Eucharist. If the Eucharist is not considered as the sum and summary of our faith, then our reasons to be a Catholic are greatly diminished.

The method of teaching our Catholic faith has changed somewhat over the past two to three generations. Before that time much teaching of the Catholic faith was done by teachers of religious orders, but as their numbers have diminished, more of such teaching has been done by lay people. In addition, the Baltimore Catechism lost its status as the teaching tool of the faith. And unfortunately, at this time in history much of the teaching does not utilize as it should, the teaching of the faith based on compendia of the Catechism of the Catholic Church. We have not done a good job of using such compendia as requested by Saint John Paul II when he released the Catechism.

As noted in Chapter 7, following Vatican II, greater emphasis was placed on other aspects of our Catholic faith and one of the unintended consequences of that was less emphasis on the important role of the Eucharist to our Catholic faith.

In regards to the Eucharist the words of St. Paul regarding the lack of faith are noteworthy at the present time. *But how can they call on him in whom they have not believed? And how can they believe in him of whom they have not heard? And how can they hear without someone to preach? And how can people preach unless they are sent?*

The Church has much work to do, to once again make the Eucharist the cornerstone of evangelization. It must start with the hierarchy of the Church and their acknowledgement that what has been done in the past few generations has not been working. The fact that only about twenty percent of baptized Catholics practice their faith after reaching adulthood should be pretty solid evidence that something needs to be changed.

The beginning of such change is going to require several steps by the hierarchy:

1. An improved and more standard approach to the teaching of the Catholic faith must be employed and greater reliance must be placed on the Catechism. As St. John Paul II noted when the Catechism was released, it is the "sure norm" and the "sure and authentic text" for teaching our Catholic faith.

2. When new or current standard compendia have been approved, our Bishops must advise all parishes that such compendia are to be used for teaching our Catholic faith.

3. Finally, and of the greatest importance, in the compendia and in teaching, our focus on the Mass and on our Sacrament of Divine Love, must be increased. It is why Catholics are Catholics, but unfortunately too many at this time are not being told that. The Miracle of the Eucharist is not understood by a large percentage of Catholics. If we can't explain why Catholics are Catholics, why should our younger generations differentiate between Christian religions or bother to attend Mass? Many of them believe they are faithful and spiritual and that should be adequate. They need to understand that He asked us to "Do This in Memory of Me" and why He asked it.

The answers to the why He asked us to "Do This in Memory of Me" are more numerous than humans can enumerate. We have reviewed some of the reasons in various parts of this book, but we will again review some of the major answers to why the Eucharist is of such great significance to our Catholic faith.

There are no events that will ever take place on earth that are of greater significance to humans beings than the Passion, Death and Resurrection of our Lord. His Crucifixion was the ultimate sacrifice that could possibly be made for each one of us. There is no greater Love that could be displayed for us.

Through his Passion, Death and Resurrection, He opened an eternal Kingdom where it is possible for us to spend eternal happiness in his presence. What He asked us to do in memory of Him is a small pittance in return for the Love He demonstrated on our behalf.

The Eucharist is of such significance to each of us that it should be our greatest desire while we are on earth. We have no greater way to unite ourselves with Him than through the reception of Holy Communion. It is our obligation to proclaim the Miracle of the Eucharist to all who will listen.

The words of our Lord are the best testimonies to the significance of the Eucharist. We have made note of most of those earlier in this book. Let us again look at a few of those words and their significance.

In the 6th Chapter of John, Jesus said: *I am the bread of life: whoever comes to me will never hunger, and who believes in me will never thirst.* In those words of the Bread of Life Discourse, Jesus is inviting us to believe in Him and that our faith in Him will make it possible for us to never hunger for greater faith and through that same faith in him we will never thirst for other beliefs.

Later in the Bread of Life Discourse of Jesus goes on to say: *Amen, amen, I say to you, whoever believes has eternal life. I am the bread of life. Your ancestors ate the manna in the desert but they died: this is the bread that comes down from heaven, so that one may eat and not die. I am the living bread that came down from heaven; whoever eats this bread will live forever; and the bread that I will give is my flesh for the life of the world.*

In those words, Jesus moved beyond just using the bread of life in a symbolic or metaphorical way, but began indicating how this might come to take place and that such bread would permit us to live forever and that He would give his flesh to us for eternal life.

After those listening to him began to quarrel among themselves as to how he could give his own flesh for us to eat, Jesus added these very direct and literal words: *Amen, amen, I say to you, unless you eat the flesh of the Son of Man and drink his blood, you do not have live within you. Whoever eats my flesh and drinks my blood has eternal life, and I will raise him on the last day. For my flesh is true food, and my blood is true drink. Whoever eats my flesh and drinks my blood remains in me and I in him.*

Those words are almost impossible to interpret in any way other than the way the Catholic Church interprets them in our Catechism which has been covered earlier. They are words that make the reception of Holy Communion the most significant of all acts we have to demonstrate our belief in Him and our love of Him. The extent of his words link heaven and earth. They link humans to his divinity. They are the words of eternal life.

On the night before He died, He went on to institute the Eucharist and to invite all of us to believe in the most special way we have - the Holy Eucharist.

If we have any hope of increasing the participation of our younger generations in their Catholic faith, we must do a better job of teaching them the miracle of the Eucharist. It will be through the Sacrament of Divine Love that they will wish to also demonstrate their love of Him, who suffered and died so they might have the opportunity to spend eternal life with Him.

CHAPTER 10

THE KEY TO
INCREASING FAITH

The Catechism of the Catholic Church states that faith is "man's response to God, who reveals himself and gives himself to man, while at the same time bringing man a superabundant light as he searches for the ultimate meaning of his life".

In both the Nicene and Apostles Creed, we begin by saying "I believe" and then we continue to profess the list of those things we do believe.

Through our faith in God, we submit our human intellect, our soul's spiritual wisdom and our free will to God. In doing that we also submit ourselves to the "obedience of faith" whereby we accept both what our Lord has revealed through Sacred Scripture and continues to reveal to us through Apostolic Tradition. It is through the obedience of faith that we open our human intellect and spiritual wisdom to a greater understanding of that faith.

When St. John Paul II issued the Catechism of the Catholic Church he noted that it served as a "sure norm" for teaching the faith and was given to the Church as a "sure and authentic reference text for teaching catholic doctrine". With Sacred Scripture and the Catechism we have the vehicles to provide us with the superabundant light we need as we search "for the ultimate meaning" of life.

With the superabundant light we also have the opportunity to grow our faith throughout the course of our life. The obedience to that ever increasing faith provides us with a growing meaning of our life.

We grow our faith in many ways and for all Christians, prayer is a common denominator of growing faith. In this book we deal with the more narrow and optimal way of growing the faith. The greater our acceptance of what Scripture and Tradition tells us of the Eucharist, the more we begin to accept and understand the special relationship it establishes between God and man. We have referred to it as The Sacrament of Divine Love. We have indicated our love of that title because the Eucharist links us with He who is Divine and is Love.

There is no greater need in the Church today, than to assist our younger generations in the understanding of the Eucharist. That understanding, as noted several times in this book, is crucial to having a greater participation in the Catholic faith. In Chapter 9, we noted the three steps the hierarchy of the Church must take to communicate a better understanding of our Catholic faith, especially the Eucharist, to all Catholics.

We titled this book, "The Miracle of the Eucharist". It is not only the transubstantiation of bread and wine into the Body, Blood, Soul and Divinity of our Lord which is a miracle. The miracle of the Eucharist extends to the linkage of our soul to our Divine Lord, whereby we share in that divinity. Divinity is itself a mystery and a miracle because it is beyond the nature of earthly things. The transformation of our souls to become more closely aligned with our Divine Lord is an extension of the miracle.

There is no greater way to increase our faith than to increase our understanding of the Eucharist and to participate as often as possible in attending the Mass and Eucharist. It is the "sum and summit of Ecclesial Life". And because it is a mystery it also transforms our soul in ways we humans cannot fully comprehend.

Hundreds of years ago, St. Robert Bellarmine wrote that there were over 200 different interpretations of Christ's words at the Last Supper that "This is my Body...This is my Blood".

I do not know how many different interpretations there are among those who profess to be Catholics, but there are certainly some who do not believe in the transubstantiation belief as noted at the Council of Trent. That belief remains the teaching of our Church today and is covered thoroughly in the Catechism.

We need to begin properly teaching our Catholic faith, beginning with the three steps noted in Chapter nine. That teaching must convey the message that there is no greater way to observe the first commandment, than the Eucharist. He makes that clear in Sacred Scripture and it is clearly stated in the Catechism. It is the way in which we love Him with all our heart, soul, mind and strength.

After we begin conveying a better understanding of the Eucharist, it is up to the faith of believers to increase their faith. There will always be some who will say as the early disciples did that this truth is too hard to believe. But there will be many more who will want to look through the divine prism of the Eucharist to increase their faith and their love of Him who died for us.

Those who will be among the people who wish to increase their faith will discover a closer association with the things of God and will find less interest in the things of the world. They will discover that unless you eat of his Flesh and drink of his Blood you do not have life within you. They will discover that it is the spirit or soul which gives life while the flesh is of no avail.

As they discover these pearls of greater holiness, they will hunger to increase their faith even more. They will go on to discover as St. John Vianney did that all the good works of men are not equal to the Holy Sacrifice of the Mass and the Eucharist. Their joy in the things of God will increase more and more. Our Love of the Lord in the Holy Eucharist will not subside, but will grow into a passionate love. That cup of love will overflow and be extended to a greater love of our neighbor.

As we grow in faith, we become more Godlike. We begin discovering that his commands, his wishes and his will become our greatest joys. Ultimately, we begin doing his will on earth as it is done in Heaven.

With increasing faith and through the Holy Eucharist, we begin appreciating the beauty and majesty of creation. We come to a better understanding of the great love He extended to each of us through his passion and death.

Each day we share in the Eucharist, we come to a greater understanding of a few of the miracles associated with a loving Holy Communion with Him. As St. Peter Julian Eymard wrote; *Until we have a passionate love for Our Lord in the most Blessed Sacrament, we shall have accomplished nothing.*

When we discover that passionate love, we shall also have discovered a greater bond between Heaven and earth, and between our soul and the Sacrament of Divine Love.

ABOUT THE AUTHOR

George E Pfautsch spent most of his working life as a financial executive for a major forest products and paper company. His final years with Potlatch Corporation were spent as the Senior Vice-President of Finance and Chief Financial Officer.

Following his retirement, he began writing about the national morality he believes was intended for this nation by the founding fathers. He is the author of eleven previous books covering the subjects of faith, freedom, morality, and justice.

In addition he is the co-author of a book written by Melitta Strandberg, which is the story of her family's quest for freedom, before, during and after World War II. He is also the co-author of a book written by Leroy New, the "Guitar Wizard" of Branson, Missouri.

George is married to Dodi, his wife of 55 years. He has two children and four grandchildren

Printed in the United States
By Bookmasters